SEMINOLE

VALERIE BODDEN

CREATIVE EDUCATION ✴ CREATIVE PAPERBACKS

Published by Creative Education and Creative Paperbacks
P.O. Box 227, Mankato, Minnesota 56002
Creative Education and Creative Paperbacks are imprints of
The Creative Company
www.thecreativecompany.us

Design by Christine Vanderbeek
Production by Colin O'Dea
Art direction by Rita Marshall
Printed in the United States of America

Photographs by Alamy (Chronicle, ClassicStock, Niday
Picture Library, Photo 12, The Protected Art Archive),
Creative Commons Wikimedia (George Catlin/anagoria,
George Catlin/Smithsonian American Art Museum, Ebyabe,
H. Charles McBarron Jr./United States Army Center of
Military History, State Library and Archives of Florida),
Getty Images (Marilyn Angel Wynn), iStockphoto (sdbower),
Shutterstock (Miloje, Steven R Smith, Emre Tarimcioglu)

Library of Congress Cataloging-in-Publication Data
Names: Bodden, Valerie, author.
Title: Seminole / Valerie Bodden.
Series: First peoples.
Includes bibliographical references and index.
Summary: An introduction to the Seminole lifestyle and
history, including their forced relocation and how they keep
traditions alive today. A Seminole story recounts why it is
important to respect traditions.
Identifiers:
ISBN 978-1-64026-227-0 (hardcover)
ISBN 978-1-62832-790-8 (pbk)
ISBN 978-1-64000-362-0 (eBook)
This title has been submitted for CIP processing under LCCN
2019939658.
CCSS: RI.1.1, 2, 3, 4, 5, 6, 7; RI.2.1, 2, 3, 4, 5, 6; RI.3.1, 2, 3, 5;
RF.1.1, 3, 4; RF.2.3, 4

First Edition HC   9 8 7 6 5 4 3 2 1
First Edition PBK   9 8 7 6 5 4 3 2 1

FIRST PEOPLES

TABLE of CONTENTS

PEOPLE OF THE EVERGLADES

The Seminole lived in what is now southern Florida. They took shelter in the wetlands of the Everglades. Their name may have come from a Creek Indian word meaning "runaway." Or it might have come from a Spanish word meaning "wild."

 Tall grasses and moss-covered trees grow thick in Florida's Everglades.

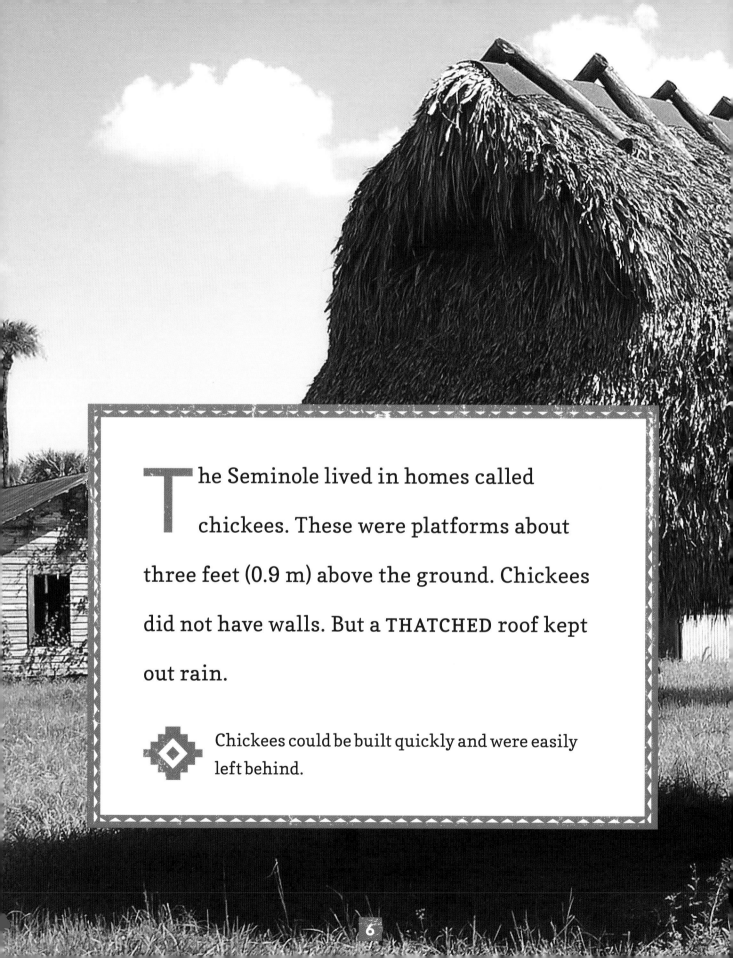

The Seminole lived in homes called chickees. These were platforms about three feet (0.9 m) above the ground. Chickees did not have walls. But a THATCHED roof kept out rain.

Chickees could be built quickly and were easily left behind.

SEMINOLE LIFE

The Seminole used canoes to get around the Everglades. They made the canoes by burning out the insides of logs. They pushed the boats through wetlands with long poles.

 The flat-bottomed dugout canoes could be 12 to 30 feet (3.7–9.1 m) long.

The Seminole grew corn and pumpkins. The women gathered wild nuts and berries. The men hunted deer, rabbits, and alligators.

 Seminole women made pottery, wove baskets, and sewed all of their family's clothing.

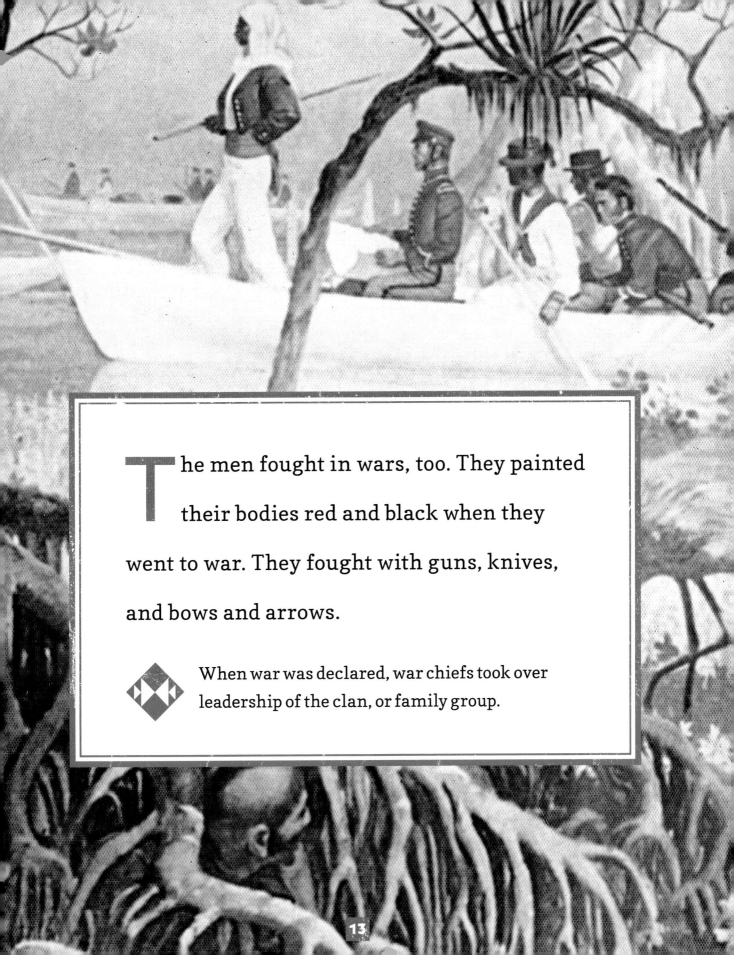

The men fought in wars, too. They painted their bodies red and black when they went to war. They fought with guns, knives, and bows and arrows.

When war was declared, war chiefs took over leadership of the clan, or family group.

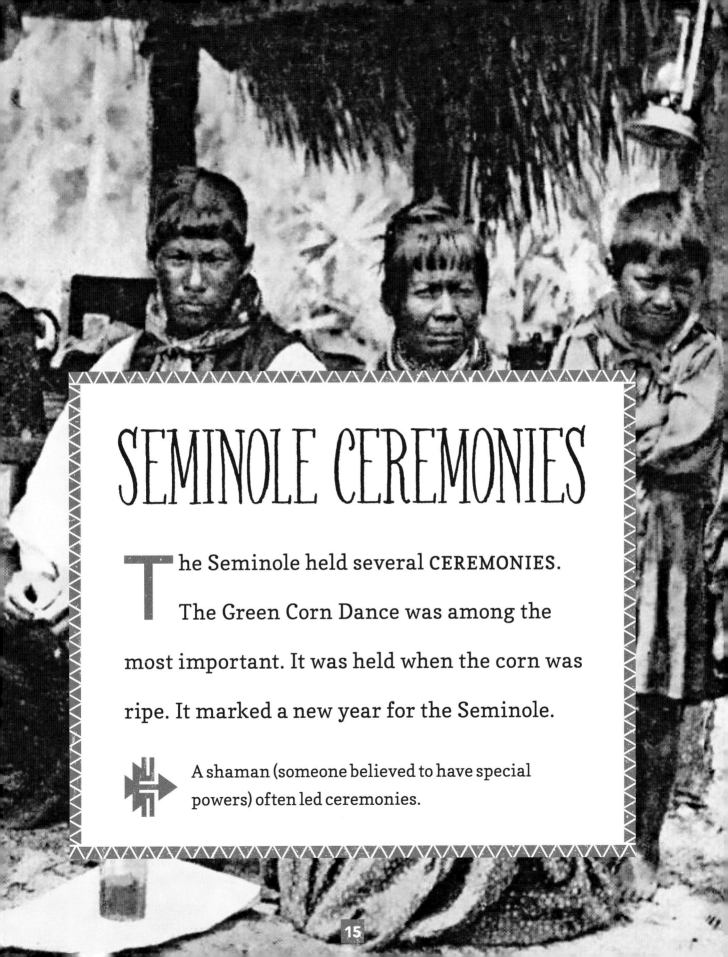

SEMINOLE CEREMONIES

The Seminole held several CEREMONIES. The Green Corn Dance was among the most important. It was held when the corn was ripe. It marked a new year for the Seminole.

A shaman (someone believed to have special powers) often led ceremonies.

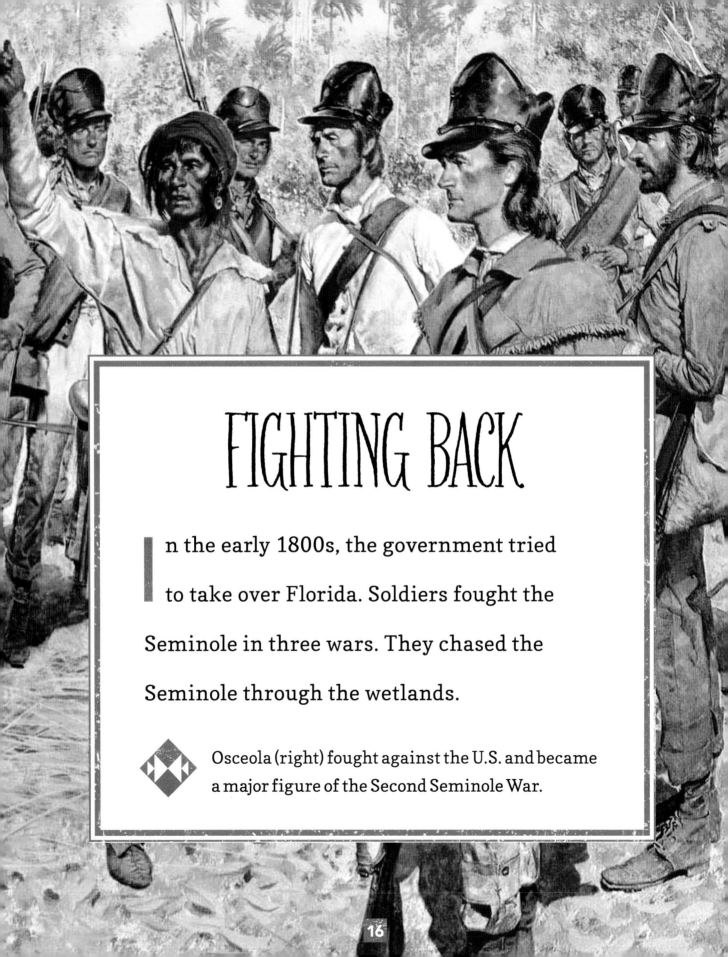

FIGHTING BACK

I n the early 1800s, the government tried to take over Florida. Soldiers fought the Seminole in three wars. They chased the Seminole through the wetlands.

Osceola (right) fought against the U.S. and became a major figure of the Second Seminole War.

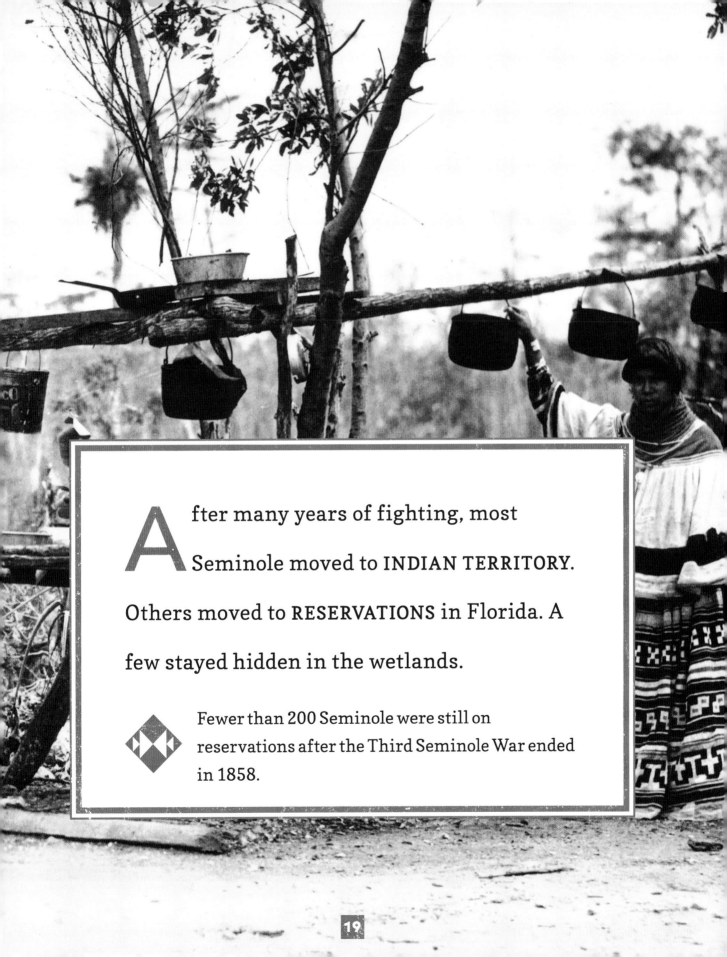

After many years of fighting, most Seminole moved to **INDIAN TERRITORY**. Others moved to **RESERVATIONS** in Florida. A few stayed hidden in the wetlands.

Fewer than 200 Seminole were still on reservations after the Third Seminole War ended in 1858.

BEING SEMINOLE

Today, most Seminole live in Oklahoma. Others live in the Everglades. Many Seminole still hold the Green Corn Dance every year. They keep their TRADITIONS alive.

 The Stomp Dance is performed several times during the Green Corn Dance.

A SEMINOLE STORY

The Seminole told stories to teach lessons. In one story, a man went for a walk. He came back with two big fish. He thought they had fallen to the ground with the rain. His friend said not to eat the fish. He did not know where they came from. But the man cooked and ate them. During the night, he turned into a snake. He knew it was because he had broken his people's law.

GLOSSARY

CEREMONIES ✦ special acts carried out according to set rules

INDIAN TERRITORY ✦ part of the United States that was set aside for American Indians; it is now the state of Oklahoma

RESERVATIONS ✦ areas of land set aside for American Indians

THATCHED ✦ describing a covering made of grasses, reeds, or other plant materials

TRADITIONS ✦ beliefs, stories, or ways of doing things that are passed down from parents to their children

READ MORE

Fullman, Joe. *Native North Americans: Dress, Eat, Write, and Play Just Like the Native Americans*. Mankato, Minn.: QEB, 2010.

Morris, Ting. *Arts and Crafts of the Native Americans*. North Mankato, Minn.: Smart Apple Media, 2007.

WEBSITES

Ah-Tah-Thi-Ki Museum
https://www.ahtahthiki.com/
Learn more about Seminole history and culture.

Seminole Tribe of Florida
https://www.semtribe.com/STOF
Find out more about the Seminole way of life.

Note: Every effort has been made to ensure that the websites listed above are suitable for children, that they have educational value, and that they contain no inappropriate material. However, because of the nature of the Internet, it is impossible to guarantee that these sites will remain active indefinitely or that their contents will not be altered.

INDEX